KNIGHTS
OF THE
ROUND TABLE

ARTHUR THE KING

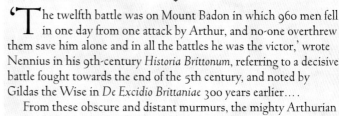

'The twelfth battle was on Mount Badon in which 960 men fell in one day from one attack by Arthur, and no-one overthrew them save him alone and in all the battles he was the victor,' wrote Nennius in his 9th-century *Historia Brittonum*, referring to a decisive battle fought towards the end of the 5th century, and noted by Gildas the Wise in *De Excidio Brittaniae* 300 years earlier....

From these obscure and distant murmurs, the mighty Arthurian tradition flows majestically towards the 21st century. Perhaps, in reality, Arthur was a 5th-century king of the Britons or merely a minor Welsh freedom fighter. Indeed, there are some who doubt his very existence, or think that he was a combination of several characters. Nevertheless, Arthur was the forerunner of King Alfred the Great, Sir Francis Drake, Admiral Lord Nelson and Sir Winston Churchill, symbolizing the resolve of Britain in peril and the unquenchable warrior spirit.

BORN TO BE KING

King Uther Pendragon had fallen passionately in love with the beautiful Ygerna, wife of Gorlois, a powerful noble living in an impregnable fortress, Tintagel, almost surrounded by the sea on the wild Cornish coast. Aided by the sorcerer Merlin, Uther magically metamorphosed into the likeness of Gorlois, easily gaining access to both the fortress and Ygerna. 'The king remained the whole night with Ygerna. That night she conceived Arthur, the most renowned of men,' records Geoffrey of Monmouth in his *History of the Kings of Britain*.

THE SWORD IN THE STONE

'There was seen in the churchyard a great stone like unto a marble stone and in the midst thereof was like an anvil of steel and therein stuck a fair sword naked by the point, and letters there were written in gold about the sword that saiden thus: "Whoso pulleth out this sword of this stone and anvil is rightwise born the King of England."'
Morte d'Arthur, *Malory*

Arthur was entrusted to Merlin, as King Uther had promised, to be brought up by the kindly old knight Ector, alongside his own son Kay.
After Uther died, Arthur, just 15 years old, was able to claim the throne, having dramatically drawn the sword from the stone after everyone else had failed. Arthur ruled over 30 kingdoms.

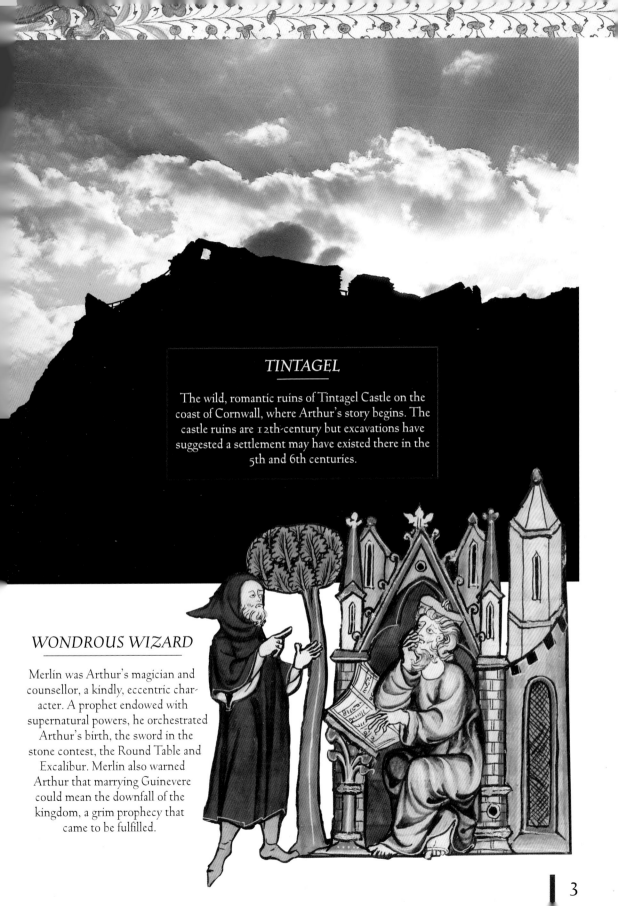

TINTAGEL

The wild, romantic ruins of Tintagel Castle on the coast of Cornwall, where Arthur's story begins. The castle ruins are 12th-century but excavations have suggested a settlement may have existed there in the 5th and 6th centuries.

WONDROUS WIZARD

Merlin was Arthur's magician and counsellor, a kindly, eccentric character. A prophet endowed with supernatural powers, he orchestrated Arthur's birth, the sword in the stone contest, the Round Table and Excalibur. Merlin also warned Arthur that marrying Guinevere could mean the downfall of the kingdom, a grim prophecy that came to be fulfilled.

KNIGHTS OF THE ROUND TABLE

Arthur drew his brotherhood of knights from far and wide. They included fearless Launcelot, loyal Bedivere, chaste Bors, brave Gawain, pure, good Perceval and bold Galahad.

The Round Table acted as the symbol and focus of their comradeship. It was the king's custom to hold court with all his knights on the major feast days of the year and before festivities commenced Arthur loved to hear the latest stirring adventure. The Round Table had originally been fashioned by the wizard Merlin for Arthur's father, Uther Pendragon. Upon his death, it came into the hands of King Leodegrance of Cameliard and when his daughter Guinevere married Arthur, the Round Table came with the new queen as part of her dowry, a table, 'round in the likeness of the world', which could seat more than 100 knights in equal status.

Arthur had commanded Merlin to find at least 50 knights 'of prowess and worship', and together with 50 more from Leodegrance, the knights sat at the table for the wedding feast of Arthur and Guinevere, all the names of the knights picked out in letters of gold. So began the fellowship of the Round Table.

THE CODE OF CHIVALRY

Under the influence of the Arthurian stories, an ideal of knightly conduct developed, requiring the knights not only to be brave and skilful in battle but also to display great powers of endurance at all times, be steadfast in adversity, modest and generous towards their fellow men, gentle and courteous to their ladies. Above all was loyalty to the king and honour for their cause. These ideals were later to be adopted by the medieval Crusaders, an élite military brotherhood of international renown. The popular tournaments of the Middle Ages provided knights with opportunities to perfect their military skills, demonstrate their bravery and compete for the attentions of the ladies.

'... It was ordained of Arthur that when his fair fellowship sat to meat their chairs should be high alike, their service equal, and none before or after his comrade. Thus no man could boast that he was exalted above his fellow, for all alike were gathered round the board, and none was alien at the breaking of Arthur's bread.'
Roman de Brut, *Robert Wace*

THE ROUND TABLE TODAY

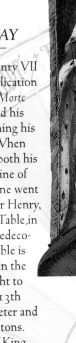

When Henry Tudor became Henry VII in 1485, shortly after the publication of Sir Thomas Malory's *Morte d'Arthur*, he emphasized his British ancestry by naming his eldest son Arthur. When Arthur died aged 16, both his young wife, Catherine of Aragon, and the throne went to his younger brother Henry, who had the Round Table in Winchester Castle redecorated. This famous table is displayed on the wall in the Great Hall. It is thought to date back to the late 13th century, is 18 feet in diameter and weighs one and a quarter tons. Henry VIII had the figure of King Arthur painted to resemble himself.

ARTHUR AND HIS KNIGHTS

The adventures of King Arthur and his knights have been chronicled by a galaxy of writers over many centuries. Kay, Bedivere, Gawain and Perceval first appeared in ancient Welsh literature, whereas Launcelot and the Quest for the Holy Grail occurred much later, in the work of Chrétien de Troyes, a French cleric and poet writing towards the end of the 12th century. Gerald of Wales, William of Malmesbury and Geoffrey of Monmouth all developed the Arthurian tradition, using many earlier sources. Geoffrey's fictional *History of the Kings of Britain*, a powerfully imaginative story which immortalized Arthur, was a best-seller in its time.

The definitive Arthurian saga, Sir Thomas Malory's *Morte d'Arthur*, describing the deeds of Arthur's many heroic knights, was written in the mid-15th century. Much later, as part of a Victorian revival of interest in Arthur, Tennyson wrote his own version of *Morte d'Arthur*, and other evocative poems such as *The Lady of Shallot* and *Idylls of the King*.

The Taking of Excalibur, J.C. Duncan.

EXCALIBUR

When Arthur broke his sword in combat, Merlin took him to a
lake where they saw a sword held above the water by a hand and
arm clad in white. The Lady of the Lake appeared, instructing them to row out and
collect the sword. 'So Arthur and Merlin dismounted and they tied their horses
to two trees and they went into the barge and when they came to the sword that the
hand held up, Arthur took it by the hilt and the hand and arm went under the
water.' (*Morte d'Arthur*, Malory). Director John Boorman's film *Excalibur* is a powerful modern portrayal of the Arthurian legend, full of romance and symbolism.

KAY – FIRST KNIGHT

Kay was Arthur's foster-brother, son of
the kindly knight Ector to whom Merlin
entrusted Arthur to be cared for as a boy.
The two were boyhood companions,
and Kay claimed that it was he who
pulled the sword from the stone; but his
father did not believe him, and insisted
that he tell the truth about Arthur.
Kay became Arthur's faithful, lifelong
servant as steward to the king's house-
hold. He was sometimes a difficult character, rough and cynical for a knight, but
always a loyal champion of the king.
Kay perished fighting with Arthur
in the war against Mordred.

CAMELOT

Camelot was the very heart of Arthur's kingdom, conjuring up the same romantic imagery as Illium or Atlantis. Here the king held court, and there were banquets, jousting, and new knights to be initiated into the fellowship of the Round Table. From Camelot the knights rode forth to seek adventure, returning at sunset to recount their achievements.

Camelot continues to be a symbol of goodness, idealism and dynamic achievement in the 20th century; when John Kennedy became the charismatic president of the USA, his Washington administration was promptly christened 'the New Camelot'.

COURT OF A KING

Numerous impressive sites have been put forward as possible places where Arthur held court. Foremost is Caerleon (below), City of the Legion, a former Roman garrison town on the River Usk in south Wales. Another former Roman centre, Chester, was also referred to as the City of the Legion. Malory favoured Winchester, probably because the Round Table hung there. Geoffrey of Monmouth proposed Tintagel as Arthur's capital, possibly to please his patron's brother, the Duke of Cornwall, as there was no evidence of a castle on the site before the 12th century.

ROMAN SITE

Viroconium, once a Roman city a few miles south-east of Shrewsbury, in Shropshire, has been most recently suggested as the site of Camelot. Viroconium (above) was once the major Roman centre in the Midlands, covering over 180 acres, ten times the size of Cadbury Hill. All that remain to be seen today are ruined walls in open countryside.

ARTHUR'S CAPITAL

Camelot was Arthur's royal stronghold, where he reigned as a benevolent high king over a joyful and peaceful kingdom, having defeated all his enemies. Arthur chose to marry Guinevere against Merlin's advice. The wise wizard prophesied that the queen's beauty would bring about the destruction of Arthur's kingdom.

THE REAL CAMELOT?

'At the very south ends of the church of South Cadbyre standith Camallate, sumtyme a famose toun or castelle, upon a very torre or hille, wunderfully enstrengtheid of nature,' marvelled Henry VIII's emissary John Leyland, writing in 1542 about Cadbury Hill in Somerset. Cadbury has been identified as a Stone Age camp, a Bronze Age fort, an Iron Age town, a Roman stronghold and, according to legend, the great court of King Arthur. On midsummer's eve, it is said that the hillside turns to glass and the king and all his knights can be seen feasting at the Round Table.

LAUNCELOT

Handsome Launcelot was the 'best of knights', regarded as the perfect chivalrous knight on a snow-white horse, the king's champion, defender of the fair and the faithful. Yet Launcelot's conduct with Guinevere betrayed King Arthur, his passion for her greater than his love of God, resulting in the failure of his Quest for the Holy Grail and finally causing the demise of the Round Table.

Launcelot was the son of King Ban of Benwick in western France. When the king died he was abandoned by his mother Elaine and brought up by the Lady of the Lake in her underwater kingdom. Introduced to the Round Table when he was 18, Launcelot was soon dazzling the court with his remarkable exploits, but then came his fateful love affair with Guinevere, which eventually led to his downfall and the destruction of Arthur's kingdom.

A BOLD KNIGHT

The story of the castle Dolorous Gard cleverly interwove Launcelot's boldness and skill in combat with overtones of inescapable impending doom. His fearless reputation was established when capturing single-handedly the hitherto impregnable castle, commanded by a shadowy, wicked tyrant, and renaming it Joyous Gard. The castle had a graveyard containing the bodies of the knights who had perished whilst attacking the fort and on the top of one massive tomb was written, 'This slab shall never be raised by the efforts of any man's hand but by him who shall conquer this Dolorous Castle and the name of that man is written here beneath.' Launcelot slowly raised the slab. Inside it said, 'Here shall lie Launcelot du Lac, the son of King Ban of Benwick.'

KING'S CHAMPION

Fearless Launcelot was Arthur's champion and right-hand man and he became the king's trusted companion. But his friendship with Arthur was marred by tragedy. Launcelot's passionate affair with the queen caused Arthur unbearable pain and led to war between the two men.

JOYOUS GARD

Bamburgh Castle, on the Northumberland coast,
reputed to be Launcelot's fairy tale castle Joyous Gard.
The fearless knight, having freed the castle from its
black curse and found the tomb inscribed there with
his name, decided to make it his home.

LAUNCELOT IN LOVE

Queen Guinevere's Maying, J. Collier.

ELAINE OF ASTALOT

Launcelot unwisely agreed to carry the colours of Elaine, the fair maid of Astalot, at a tournament in Camelot. Elaine was 'So hot in her love that she besought to wear upon him at the joust some token of hers.' (*Morte d'Arthur*, Malory). Elaine boldly asked Launcelot to marry her and when he chivalrously declined she begged him to let her become his mistress. Again Launcelot turned her down, whereupon the despairing Elaine starved herself to death and floated down the river on a barge to Camelot, embarrassing Launcelot and infuriating Queen Guinevere, who was very jealous.

'Then Sir Launcelot began to resort unto Queen Guinevere again and forgot the promise and the perfection.' (*Morte d'Arthur*, Malory).

The beautiful Guinevere proved a troublesome wife to King Arthur. Her tempestuous affair with Launcelot scandalized the royal court.

Guinevere was repeatedly abducted from Camelot by wicked knights, firstly by Meleagaunt, then Gasozein followed by Valerin, King of the Tangled Wood and finally by Arthur's evil illegitimate son Mordred. The fearless Launcelot undertook many adventures to rescue Guinevere. Launcelot is seen, right, in combat with Meleagaunt, while Guinevere and Meleagaunt's father Badgdemus look on.

Lying, robed in snowy white
that loosely flew to left and right
the leaves upon her falling light
thro' the noises of the night
she floated down to Camelot
and as the boat head wound along
the willowy hills and fields among
they heard her singing her last song
the Lady of Shallot.

The Lady of Shallot, *Tennyson*

The Lady of Shallot, J.W. Waterhouse.

ELAINE OF CORBENIC

Another fair maiden who fell in love with Launcelot was King Pelles' daughter, Elaine of Corbenic. An enchantress tricked Launcelot into making love to Elaine, in the belief that she was Guinevere. When Launcelot discovered the truth he forgave her, 'for she was a fair lady and thereto lusty and young, and wise as any that was at that time living.' (*Morte d'Arthur*, Malory). This brief encounter resulted in the birth of a son. 'As soon as her time came, she was delivered of a fair child and they christened him Galahad.' (*Morte d'Arthur*, Malory).

LAUNCELOT'S BETRAYAL

'… *And ever stood Sir Agravain and Sir Mordred crying, 'traitor knight come out of the Queen's chamber.'*'
Morte d'Arthur, *Malory*

These two unhappy knights spied on Launcelot and Guinevere's affair and revealed their disloyalty to King Arthur. This led irrevocably to the destruction of the Round Table fellowship. When the dark knight Mordred and his followers surprised Launcelot in the queen's bedchamber he was forced to flee, yet returned to rescue Guinevere from a charge of treason, which carried the penalty of being burnt at the stake. During the ensuing flight, Launcelot killed Gawain's brothers, thereby dividing the loyalties of the Knights of the Round Table.

Launcelot retreated first to Joyous Gard, then to France. When he eventually returned to England, Arthur was dead, Guinevere in a convent. Launcelot briefly became a hermit but on hearing the news of Guinevere's death his heart could take no more, and he died.

The Arming and Departure of Knights, E. Burne-Jones.

THE KNIGHTS' JOURNEY

It was the Feast of Pentecost at Camelot, King Arthur and all his knights were gathered at the Round Table ready to dine when suddenly '... The Holy Grail appeared, covered in white samite [a rich silk fabric sometimes interwoven with gold]. No one could see who carried it. It entered through the Great Door and immediately the hall was filled with fragrance, as if all the spices of the earth had been scattered there. The Holy Grail passed through the hall, around each table, and where it passed, whatever each knight desired to eat, it appeared in his place. Then when everyone had been served, the Holy Grail disappeared.' (*La Queste del Saint Graal*, Anon).

Gawain vowed that he would leave the following morning in pursuit of the Holy Grail, and the remaining knights swore a collective oath to do the same. The king and all the ladies of the court were greatly troubled, fearing that many knights would perish and not return to Camelot, yet they were powerless to prevent this great mission.

So at first light the knights arose and, after Mass, embraced the king and their loved ones before riding out from Camelot.

GALAHAD

'My strength is as the strength of ten because my heart is pure', wrote Tennyson of Galahad. The mysticism surrounding King Arthur and the Knights of the Round Table culminated in the perfect knight Galahad and the Quest for the Holy Grail. The bold Galahad superseded his father Launcelot as 'the best of knights', possessing all Launcelot's skill in combat yet having a chaste and upright character that was beyond temptation.

Galahad alone embodied the finest attributes of chivalry: love, honour and unswerving loyalty. These virtues lasted throughout his lifetime, while misadventure befell all around him. His reward was to be the only knight privileged to discover the true meaning of the Holy Grail.

◆

'But all my heart is drawn above,
my knees are bow'd in crypt and shrine
I never felt the kiss of love
nor maiden's hand in mine.'

Tennyson

Sir Galahad, A.F. Watts.

NOBLE KNIGHT

'In the meanwhile came in a good old man, and an ancient clothed all in white, and there was no knight knew from whence he came. And with him he brought a young knight, both on foot, in red arms, without sword or shield, save a scabbard hanging by his side. And these words he said: "Peace be with you, fair lords."'
(*Morte d'Arthur*, Malory).
Thus was Galahad led into Arthur's court and given a white shield with a red cross.

THE HOLY GRAIL

According to legend, Joseph of Arimathea used the vessel from The Last Supper to collect Christ's blood at the Crucifixion. When Christ rose from the dead he came to Joseph and taught him the vessel's true meaning. Many centuries later Chrétien de Troyes, Robert de Boron and the unnamed Cistercian writers of the Vulgate Cycle were to describe the vessel which Joseph is reputed to have brought to Glastonbury as a *graal*, meaning a deep serving-dish in Old French, translating into English as 'grail'. Whether a serving-dish, cup or chalice, the Grail possessed a unique connection with the Son of God and held such a powerful religious significance for the Christian knights of Arthur's Round Table that it provided the cornerstone for the Arthurian story.

How an angel rowed Sir Galahad across Dern Mere, N. Paton.

BORS – MODEST KNIGHT

Bors' character was as good, pure and modest as Galahad's. When he courteously rebuffed the advances of a fair lady, she threatened to jump off the top of a tower with all her ladies-in-waiting. Bors watched impassively as they hurtled to their deaths. Bors was a survivor. He came unscathed through the perilous Quest for the Holy Grail and the terrible Battle of Camlann, later travelling to the Holy Land to take part in the Crusades. Fate chose him to accompany Perceval and Galahad on the Grail Quest, showing that goodness achieves its own reward, a central theme of the story of the Grail.

QUEST FOR THE HOLY GRAIL

Gawain came close to finding the elusive Grail but failed in the end, as did Launcelot, because only those who were free from sin could achieve such a difficult goal. Many of the knights were inspired to go on the quest, but it was a hazardous journey and many perished despite their bravery.

Perceval, Bors and Galahad finally found the Grail at the castle of the maimed Fisher King, a character associated with an early, probably Celtic, fertility story. Perceval had visited him previously but failed to ask the vital question, 'What is the Grail and whom does it serve?', which would have healed the king's wound and restored his barren land to fertility. The three knights took the Grail to the Holy Land, where its true secret was revealed only to the saintly Galahad. Galahad gazed into the sacred vessel, discovered its divine truth and died in perfect peace, requesting of Bors, 'Remember me to my father, Sir Launcelot.'

The Quest for the Holy Grail, E. Burne-Jones (above and below).

ORIGINS OF THE GRAIL QUEST

The story of the Quest for the Holy Grail was developed in the aftermath of the fall of Jerusalem to the Muslim leader Saladin in 1187.
At this time Richard the Lionheart, Frederick Barbarossa and many other great European leaders embarked on the Third Crusade to recapture the Holy City for Christendom. Richard gave a sword, supposedly Arthur's, to Tancred, the ruler of Sicily. The great medieval warriors, such as the Lionheart, resembled Arthur's knights, just as the Crusades mirrored the Grail Quest. The Knights Templar (crusading knights who protected pilgrims on the road to the Holy City) saw themselves as keepers of the Grail, and wore white surcoats with a red cross, similar to Galahad's shield.

THE FISHER KING

Bran, a hero of Welsh legend, is suggested by some sources to be the Fisher King, keeper of the Grail. His castle is identified as Castell Dinas Bran, at Llangollen, in Clwyd, the remains of a 13th-century castle built inside an iron-age hillfort.

GAWAIN

'One of the most faultless of fellows', Gawain was eldest son of King Lot of the Orkneys and Morgause, Arthur's half-sister. He was a mighty warrior with an ability to multiply his strength three times before noon. At one time he had been Launcelot's closest friend, but Launcelot killed three of his brothers which made him Gawain's most bitter enemy. Eventually the pair met in single combat and after a titanic struggle, Gawain received a blow to the head which later proved fatal. Gawain's ghost appeared to Arthur before the Battle of Camlann warning him not to fight Mordred but to seek a peaceful solution.

The story of Gawain and the Green Knight is one of a quartet of poems by an unknown, yet gifted, writer of the late 14th century. One of the literary masterpieces of its time, the story skilfully dovetails two classic themes, fortitude in the face of a supernatural threat and resisting temptation. The story was deliberately ironic. By the Middle Ages, Gawain's immense bravery remained undoubted but he had acquired a reputation as a great womaniser.

PERCEVAL – A PURE KNIGHT

Perceval, a simple country boy, led an extremely sheltered life. When he first encountered some knights, he thought they were angels because of their shining armour. He was brought up by his mother, whose husband and two elder sons had died violent deaths, and she was therefore determined to protect Perceval from harm. Perceval was so naïve that when he became a knight he was nicknamed 'The Perfect Fool', but a brave heart and a pure mind ensured that Perceval was chosen, together with Bors and Galahad, to undertake the hazardous Quest for the Holy Grail.

GAWAIN AND THE GREEN KNIGHT

It was New Year's Day. Arthur and his court were feasting at Camelot when in strode an awesome giant of a knight. He was bright green from head to toe: hair, skin, clothes, even his horse was green and he carried a massive green axe.
The Green Knight challenged anyone to freely strike off his head, providing they would accept a similar fate in a year's time. Gawain accepted the challenge and with one fearsome blow severed the Green Knight's head. To everyone's horror, the Green Knight calmly picked it up and, reminding Gawain to meet him in a year's time, galloped off with his own head tucked under his arm.
The following Christmas, while searching for the Green Chapel where the challenge was to be renewed, Gawain spied a splendid castle whose genial owner invited him to stay. The following day, he asked Gawain to accompany him on a hunting trip but Gawain, exhausted by his journey, decided to stay in bed, whereupon the owner's ravishing wife appeared, and invited him to her bed.
To her surprise, Gawain declined. These events occurred repeatedly. Once more seeking the Green Chapel, Gawain by chance encountered the Green Knight. He bowed his head and gallantly awaited his fate. Three times the axe descended, three times it was checked just in time – for the ferocious Green Knight was really the urbane owner of the castle, and the entire episode merely a test of Gawain's knightly virtues.

TWO LUCKY ESCAPES

Perceval was fortunate to escape with his life when his horse was killed in a skirmish with 20 knights. He was saved by Galahad, who chased off the enemy. Perceval's greatest challenge was resisting the charms of the fair maiden who fed him a lavish feast before attempting to seduce him. She very nearly succeeded, though Perceval's virtue survived unscathed.

TRISTAN & ISOLDE

T ristan was the clever, handsome
nephew of King Mark of Cornwall,
highly talented in the courtly pursuits
of hunting, jousting and dancing, and
also excelling at singing and playing the
harp. King Mark sent Tristan to Ireland
to bring back the lovely Princess Isolde
whom the king intended to marry.
Upon his arrival in Ireland, brave
Tristan fought and killed a dragon.
The monster wounded him and Isolde
nursed him. Isolde's mother entrusted
the ladies-in-waiting with a love potion
to be given to King Mark and Isolde
to ensure a happy marriage. On the
voyage to Cornwall, the potion was
mistakenly given to Tristan and Isolde,
and they fell passionately in love.

DOOMED LOVERS

For several years the couple's illicit affair remained
unnoticed, but when the king finally discovered their
secret, Tristan was forced to leave Cornwall. He
became a Knight of the Round Table and travelled to
Brittany where he met and married another Isolde,
named Isolde of the White Hands. Tristan, however,
still loved his first Isolde, so when he was dangerously
wounded fighting the evil knight Estult L'Orgillus, he
sent for the princess, requesting that her ship should
carry a white sail. When the ship arrived, Tristan's
jealous wife told him that the sail was black.
The mortally wounded Tristan lost heart and
died before the princess reached him.
'She embraced him and lying beside him on the bed,
she kissed his lips and face, clasping him tightly in her
arms, body to body, mouth to mouth, she gave up her
spirit at that moment and died beside her beloved for
sorrow at his death.' (*Tristan*, Thomas d'Angleterre).
Their bodies were brought back to
Cornwall by King Mark and buried at
Tintagel. A vine and a rose grew out of
the grave and entwined the bodies
tightly together, lovers embraced in
death, eternally inseparable.

How, as they sailed towards Cornwall, they saw on a day the flasket wherein was the love-filtre which
the Queen of Ireland was sending by the hand of Dame Brangwaine for Isoude to drink with King
Mark, and how Tristram drank it with her, both unwitting and how they loved each other ever after

How Sir Tristram & King Mark were made at one again by King Arthur: means how nevertheless King Mark
slew Sir Tristram by treachery as he sat harping to La Belle Isoude: Isoude died the third day after

WAGNER'S TRAGIC TALE

The Arthurian love stories, intense, poignant, invariably ending in tragedy, provided superb operatic material for Richard Wagner, the 19th-century German composer. His great opera *Tristan and Isolde*, composed in 1871, was inspired by the tragic couple's doomed tale. His last opera, *Parsifal*, first performed in 1882, told the story of the good knight Perceval.

Tristan and Iseult, J.M.Strudwick.

LYONESSE

St Michael's Mount, off the Cornish coast, part of the legendary lost kingdom of Lyonesse, which extended to the Isles of Scilly. Tristan was a prince of Lyonesse, which was flooded by Merlin to drown Mordred's knights as they pursued Arthur's army after the Battle of Camlann.

MORDRED

◆

Mordred was born of a brief liaison between Arthur and his half-sister Morgause. This dark knight eventually caused the destruction of the Round Table and the death of Arthur. Mordred was originally one of Arthur's knights and a trusted companion of Launcelot, but the dark side of his nature emerged when he realised that Launcelot and Guinevere's illicit love could bring down the kingdom, and he exposed their affair to the king. Launcelot fled to France with a vengeful Arthur in pursuit, having appointed Mordred his regent. After abducting Guinevere, Mordred tried to usurp the kingdom. Arthur and his army returned to Britain to confront Mordred's massed troops at Camlann for a final apocalyptic battle.

◆

WICKED SISTERS

Arthur was mischievously seduced by Morgause, his voluptuous half-sister and wife of King Lot of the Orkneys, without him knowing her true identity. The union resulted in the birth of Mordred. Arthur's other wicked half-sister, Morgan le Fay, harboured an obsessive hatred for the king, his father Uther Pendragon having slain her mother's first husband Gorlois, father to both Morgan and Morgause. Merlin had taught Morgan le Fay magical powers, including the ability to fly and to change shape at will. She used sorcery to pursue Arthur relentlessly throughout his reign.

Morgan le Fay, A.F.Sandys.

THE LAST BATTLE

'When Sir Mordred heard King Arthur, he ran towards him with his sword drawn in his hand. And there King Arthur smote Sir Mordred under the shield, with a thrust of his spear more than a fathom through the body. And when Sir Mordred felt that he had his death wound, he thrust himself with the might that he had up to the bur of King Arthur's spear. And right so he smote his father Arthur, with his sword held in both his hands, on the side of the head, that the sword pierced the helmet and the brain pan. Therewith Sir Mordred fell stark dead to the earth; and the noble Arthur fell. ...'
Morte d'Arthur, Malory

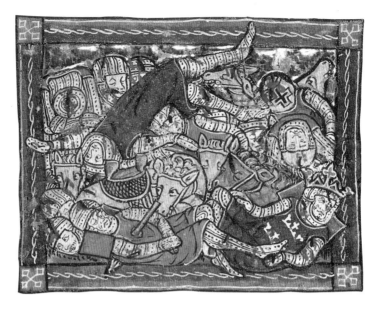

BEDIVERE – THE LAST KNIGHT

The one-handed Bedivere was the only one of Arthur's close companions still with him after the Battle of Camlann. The usually depend-
able Bedivere was entrusted to return the enchanted sword, Excalibur,
to the lake, yet so reluctant was he that Arthur had to send him back
twice. When Bedivere finally cast the sword into the lake, an arm clad
in white silk rose above the surface, caught it, brandished it three
times and vanished into the depths. Dozmary Pool (below right), on
Bodmin Moor in Cornwall, is thought to be the legendary lake.

Arthur's Final Days

'For I will unto the Isle of Avalon to heal me of my grievous wound and if thou never hear of me more, pray for my soul.'
Morte d'Arthur, *Malory*

◆

After Bedivere had cast Arthur's sword into the lake, a barge appeared containing a number of black-hooded women, including the king's half-sister Morgan le Fay. Bedivere gently placed Arthur in the barge and watched it slowly disappear towards Avalon where the horrific wounds Arthur had sustained at Camlann could be nursed by Morgan le Fay and her helpers. Arthur was reconciled with his formerly treacherous half-sister in his dying hours. Thereafter the king was never seen again.

◆

ARTHUR'S GRAVE

During rebuilding work in 1190 at Glastonbury Abbey, a mere ten miles from Cadbury Hill, the monks claimed to have unearthed a stone slab inscribed, 'Here lies the renowned King Arthur in the Isle of Avalon.' Below was a wooden coffin containing the bones of a tall man with a badly damaged skull. The monks were much in need of funds for the abbey. Their great patron King Henry II had just died, and the new king was away on the Crusades. The dramatic discovery helped to put Glastonbury on the map, attracting large numbers of pilgrims.

The Death of Arthur, J. Archer.

'… yet some men say in many parts of England that King Arthur is not dead, but had by the will of Our Lord Jesu into another place; and men say that he shall come again, and he shall win the Holy Cross. I will not say that it shall be so but rather I will say, here in this world he changed his life. But many men say that there is written upon his tomb this verse: "Hic iacet Arthurus, rex quondam, rexque futurus" ['Here lies Arthur, once and future king.']' Morte d'Arthur, *Malory*

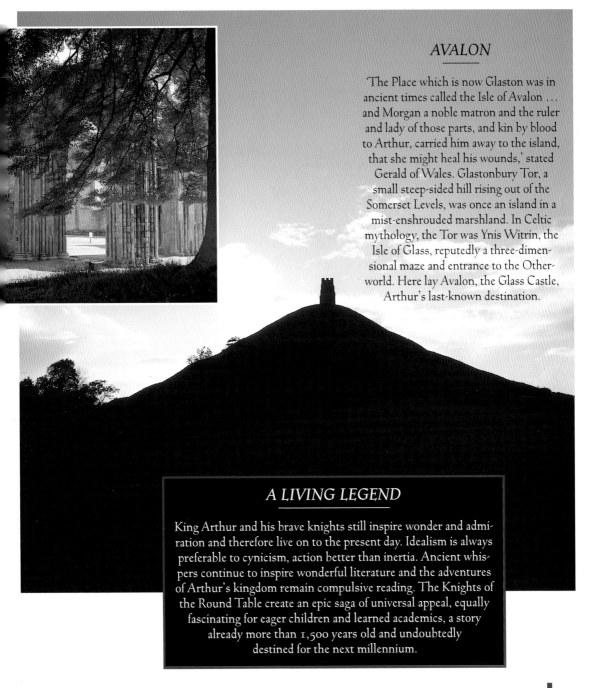

AVALON

'The Place which is now Glaston was in ancient times called the Isle of Avalon … and Morgan a noble matron and the ruler and lady of those parts, and kin by blood to Arthur, carried him away to the island, that she might heal his wounds,' stated Gerald of Wales. Glastonbury Tor, a small steep-sided hill rising out of the Somerset Levels, was once an island in a mist-enshrouded marshland. In Celtic mythology, the Tor was Ynis Witrin, the Isle of Glass, reputedly a three-dimensional maze and entrance to the Otherworld. Here lay Avalon, the Glass Castle, Arthur's last-known destination.

A LIVING LEGEND

King Arthur and his brave knights still inspire wonder and admiration and therefore live on to the present day. Idealism is always preferable to cynicism, action better than inertia. Ancient whispers continue to inspire wonderful literature and the adventures of Arthur's kingdom remain compulsive reading. The Knights of the Round Table create an epic saga of universal appeal, equally fascinating for eager children and learned academics, a story already more than 1,500 years old and undoubtedly destined for the next millennium.

PLACES TO VISIT

ARTHUR'S BIRTHPLACE

Reputed to be Tintagel in north Cornwall, where Uther Pendragon seduced Ygerna and subsequently married her, following the death of her husband. Beneath the headland of the castle lies Merlin's cave.

ARTHUR AND GUINEVERE'S GRAVE

Marked with a plaque within Glastonbury Abbey, ruined since the Dissolution of the Monasteries in 1539, when the last abbot was dragged up Glastonbury Tor to be hanged, drawn and quartered.

AVALON

After the Battle of Camlann, Arthur is said to have been taken to Glastonbury Tor, now a steep-sided hill on the edge of the town of Glastonbury, in Somerset, thought to have been the Isle of Avalon.

BADON

The battlefield where Arthur's army decisively defeated the Saxons in AD 493 is most popularly located at Little Solsbury Hill near Bath (Badanceaster, city of Badan in the *Anglo-Saxon Chronicles*). Alternative sites are Badbury Rings, between Blandford Forum and Wimborne Minster in Dorset, or Liddington Castle, close to Badbury near Swindon, in Wiltshire.

BARDSEY ISLAND (*pictured right*)

Situated off the tip of Lleyn Peninsula in north-west Wales. According to legend, Merlin still lives there.

BRITTANY

The Centre de l'Imaginaire Arthurien at Comper-en-Brocéliande (near Paimpont) organizes exhibitions and events to promote interest in the Arthurian and Celtic legends.

CAERLEON

On the River Usk in south Wales, near Newport, is the ruined remains of a splendid former Roman town and a possible site of King Arthur's Court.

CAMELOT

Arthur's fabled city, thought to be at Cadbury Hill, once an iron-age fort (just off the A303 at South Cadbury), near the villages of West Camel and Queen's Camel in Somerset. Recent excavations have shown that the site had been re-occupied and extensively fortified at the time that Arthur is supposed to have lived.

CAMLANN

Arthur's last battle, variously located on Salisbury Plain, at Slaughter Bridge near Camelford in Cornwall, at Birdoswald on Hadrian's Wall above the River Irthing, or in an isolated valley five miles east of Dolgellau in Wales at a place actually named Camlan.

DOZMARY POOL

An isolated lake on Bodmin Moor in Cornwall, a favoured spot where Bedivere cast away Excalibur after the Battle of Camlann. A more recently suggested alternative is the Berth Pool near Baschurch in Shropshire, just north-west of Shrewsbury.

JOYOUS GARD

Malory speculated that either Bamburgh or nearby Alnwick Castle, the seat of the Duke of Northumberland in north-eastern England, could originally have been Launcelot's castle Joyous Gard.

KING ARTHUR'S LABYRINTH

A superb underground 'dark-ride' exhibition about Arthur, located at the Braich Goch Slate Mine in the Corris Valley at the northern end of the magnificent Cader Idris in Wales.

THE ROUND TABLE

Displayed in the 12th-century Great Hall, all that remains of Winchester Castle, originally built by William the Conqueror. Malory also locates Camelot there. Winchester was formerly a Saxon capital.

STONEHENGE

Magically placed on Salisbury Plain by Merlin as a memorial to valiant warriors, according to the ever-ingenious Geoffrey of Monmouth.

VIROCONIUM

More recently proposed as the true capital of Arthur's kingdom, a former Roman city, now only ruins, close to Shrewsbury, in Shropshire.